Francis Frith's
Buckinghamshire

Photographic Memories

Francis Frith's

Buckinghamshire

Revised edition of original work by

Martin Andrew

FRITH BOOK Co

Revised paperback edition published in the United Kingdom in 2000 by
Frith Book Company Ltd

First published in the United Kingdom in 1998
by WBC Ltd

British Library Cataloguing in Publication Data

Francis Frith's Buckinghamshire
Martin Andrew

ISBN 1-85937-200-7

Frith Book Company Ltd
Frith's Barn, Teffont,
Salisbury, Wiltshire SP3 5QP
Tel: +44 (0) 1722 716 376
Email: info@frithbook.co.uk
www.frithbook.co.uk

Printed and bound in Great Britain

Front Cover: Chesham, High Street 1921 70538

Contents

Francis Frith: *Victorian Pioneer*

FRANCIS FRITH, Victorian founder of the world-famous photographic archive, was a complex and multitudinous man. A devout Quaker and a highly successful Victorian businessman, he was both philosophic by nature and pioneering in outlook.

By 1855 Francis Frith had already established a wholesale grocery business in Liverpool, and sold it for the astonishing sum of £200,000, which is the equivalent today of over £15,000,000. Now a multi-millionaire, he was able to indulge his passion for travel. As a child he had pored over travel books written by early explorers, and his fancy and imagination had been stirred by family holidays to the sublime mountain regions of Wales and Scotland. 'What a land of spirit-stirring and enriching scenes and places!' he had written. He was to return to these scenes of grandeur in later years to 'recapture the thousands of vivid and tender memories', but with a different purpose. Now in his thirties, and captivated by the new science of photography, Frith set out on a series of pioneering journeys to the Nile regions that occupied him from 1856 until 1860.

Intrigue and Adventure

He took with him on his travels a specially-designed wicker carriage that acted as both dark-room and sleeping chamber. These far-flung journeys were packed with intrigue and adventure. In his life story, written when he was sixty-three, Frith tells of being held captive by bandits, and of fighting 'an awful midnight battle to the very point of surrender with a deadly pack of hungry, wild dogs'. Sporting flowing Arab costume, Frith arrived at Akaba by camel seventy years before Lawrence, where he encountered 'desert princes and rival sheikhs, blazing with jewel-hilted swords'.

During these extraordinary adventures he was assiduously exploring the desert regions bordering the Nile and patiently recording the antiquities and peoples with his camera. He was the first photographer to venture beyond the sixth cataract. Africa was still the mysterious 'Dark Continent', and Stanley and Livingstone's historic meeting was a decade into the future. The conditions for picture taking confound belief. He laboured for hours in his wicker dark-room in the sweltering heat of the desert, while the volatile chemicals fizzed dangerously in their trays. Often he was forced to work in remote tombs and caves where conditions were cooler. Back in London he exhibited his photographs and was 'rapturously cheered' by members of the Royal Society. His reputation as a photographer was made overnight. An eminent modern historian has likened their impact on the population of the time to that on our own generation of the first photographs taken on the surface of the moon.

Venture of a Life-Time

Characteristically, Frith quickly spotted the opportunity to create a new business as a specialist publisher of photographs. He lived in an era of immense and sometimes violent change. For the poor in the early part of Victoria's reign work was a drudge and the hours long, and people had precious little free time to enjoy themselves. Most had no transport other than a cart or gig at their disposal, and had not travelled far beyond the boundaries of their own town or village. However, by the 1870s, the railways had threaded their way across the country, and Bank Holidays and half-day Saturdays had been made obligatory by Act of Parliament. All of a sudden the ordinary working man and his family were able to enjoy days out and see a little more of the world.

With characteristic business acumen, Francis Frith foresaw that these new tourists would enjoy having souvenirs to commemorate their days out. In 1860 he married Mary Ann Rosling and set out with the intention of photographing every city, town and village in Britain. For the next thirty years he travelled the country by train and by pony and trap, producing fine photographs of seaside resorts and beauty spots that were keenly bought by millions of Victorians. These prints were painstakingly pasted into family albums and pored over during the dark nights of winter, rekindling precious memories of summer excursions.

The Rise of Frith & Co

Frith's studio was soon supplying retail shops all over the country. To meet the demand he gathered about him a small team of photographers, and published the work of independent artist-photographers of the calibre of Roger Fenton and Francis Bedford. In order to gain some understanding of the scale of Frith's business one only has to look at the catalogue issued by Frith & Co in 1886: it runs to some 670 pages, listing not only many thousands of views of the British Isles but also many photographs of most European countries, and China, Japan, the USA and

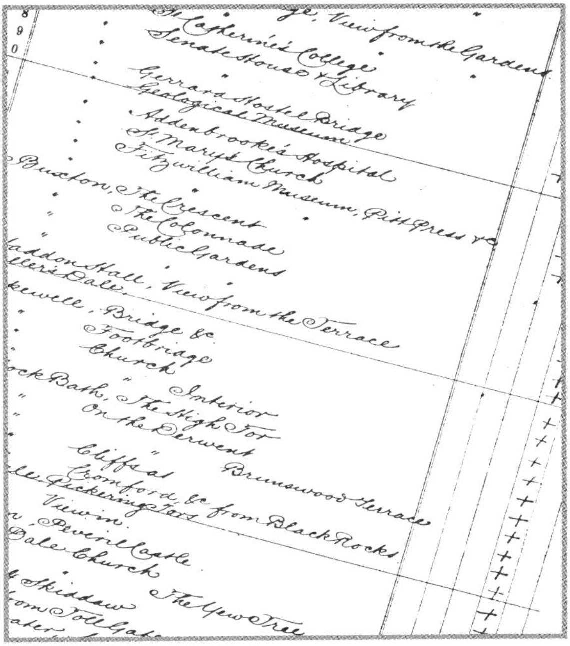
St Catherine's College, View from the Gardens
Senate House & Library
Gerrard Hostel Bridge
Geological Museum
Addenbrooke's Hospital
St Mary's Church
Fitzwilliam Museum, Pitt Press &c
Buxton, The Crescent
The Colonnade
Public Gardens
addon Hall, View from the Terrace
llers Dale
kewell, Bridge &c
Footbridge
Church
ck Bath, " Interior
The High Tor
On the Derwent
Cliffs at " Brunswood Terrace
Cromford, &c from Black Rocks
Pickering Tors
View in
Peveril Castle
Dale Church
Skiddaw The Yew Tree

Canada – note the sample page shown above from the hand-written *Frith & Co* ledgers detailing pictures taken. By 1890 Frith had created the greatest specialist photographic publishing company in the world, with over 2,000 outlets – more than the combined number that Boots and WH Smith have today! The picture on the right shows the *Frith & Co* display board at Ingleton in the Yorkshire Dales. Beautifully constructed with mahogany frame and gilt inserts, it could display up to a dozen local scenes.

Postcard Bonanza

The ever-popular holiday postcard we know today took many years to develop. In 1870 the Post Office issued the first plain cards, with a pre-printed stamp on one face. In 1894 they allowed other publishers' cards to be sent through the mail with an attached adhesive halfpenny stamp. Demand grew rapidly, and in 1895 a new size of postcard was permitted called the court card, but there was little room for illustration. In 1899, a year after Frith's death, a new card measuring 5.5 x 3.5 inches became the standard format, but it was not until 1902 that the divided back came into being, with address and message on one face and a full-size illustration on the other. *Frith & Co* were in the vanguard of postcard development, and Frith's sons Eustace and Cyril continued their father's monumental task, expanding the number of views offered to the public and recording more and more places in Britain, as the coasts and countryside were opened up to mass travel.

Francis Frith died in 1898 at his villa in Cannes, his great project still growing. The archive he created continued in business for another seventy years. By 1970 it contained over a third of a million pictures of 7,000 cities, towns and villages. The massive photographic record Frith has left to us stands as a living monument to a special and very remarkable man.

Frith's Archive: *A Unique Legacy*

FRANCIS FRITH'S legacy to us today is of immense significance and value, for the magnificent archive of evocative photographs he created provides a unique record of change in 7,000 cities, towns and villages throughout Britain over a century and more. Frith and his fellow studio photographers revisited locations many times down the years to update their views, compiling for us an enthralling and colourful pageant of British life and character.

We tend to think of Frith's sepia views of Britain as nostalgic, for most of us use them to conjure up memories of places in our own lives with which we have family associations. It often makes us forget that to Francis Frith they were records of daily life as it was actually being lived in the cities, towns and villages of his day. The Victorian age was one of great and often bewildering change for ordinary people, and though the pictures evoke an impression of slower times, life was as busy and hectic as it is today.

We are fortunate that Frith was a photographer of the people, dedicated to recording the minutiae of everyday life. For it is this sheer wealth of visual data, the painstaking chronicle of changes in dress, transport, street layouts, buildings, housing, engineering and landscape that captivates us so much today. His remarkable images offer us a powerful link with the past and with the lives of our ancestors.

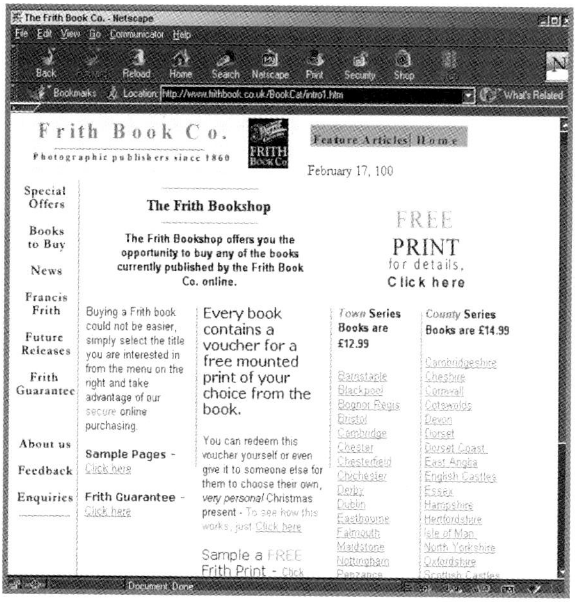

See Frith at www. frithbook.co.uk

Today's Technology

Computers have now made it possible for Frith's many thousands of images to be accessed almost instantly. In the Frith archive today, each photograph is carefully 'digitised' then stored on a CD Rom. Frith archivists can locate a single photograph amongst thousands within seconds. Views can be catalogued and sorted under a variety of categories of place and content to the immediate benefit of researchers.

Inexpensive reference prints can be created for them at the touch of a mouse button, and a wide range of books and other printed materials assembled and published for a wider, more general readership - in the next twelve months over a hundred Frith local history titles will be published! The day-to-day workings of the archive are very different from how they were in Francis Frith's time: imagine the herculean task of sorting through eleven tons of glass negatives as Frith had to do to locate a particular sequence of pictures! Yet the archive still prides itself on maintaining the same high standards of excellence laid down by Francis Frith, including the painstaking cataloguing and indexing of every view.

It is curious to reflect on how the internet now allows researchers in America and elsewhere greater instant access to the archive than Frith himself ever enjoyed. Many thousands of individual views can be called up on screen within seconds on one of the Frith internet sites, enabling people living continents away to revisit the streets of their ancestral home town, or view places in Britain where they have enjoyed holidays. Many overseas researchers welcome the chance to view special theme selections, such as transport, sports, costume and ancient monuments.

We are certain that Francis Frith would have heartily approved of these modern developments in imaging techniques, for he himself was always working at the very limits of Victorian photographic technology.

The Value of the Archive Today

Because of the benefits brought by the computer, Frith's images are increasingly studied by social historians, by researchers into genealogy and ancestory, by architects, town planners, and by teachers and schoolchildren involved in local history projects.

In addition, the archive offers every one of us an opportunity to examine the places where we and our families have lived and worked down the years. Highly successful in Frith's own era, the archive is now, a century and more on, entering a new phase of popularity.

The Past in Tune with the Future

Historians consider the Francis Frith Collection to be of prime national importance. It is the only archive of its kind remaining in private ownership and has been valued at a million pounds. However, this figure is now rapidly increasing as digital technology enables more and more people around the world to enjoy its benefits.

Francis Frith's archive is now housed in an historic timber barn in the beautiful village of Teffont in Wiltshire. Its founder would not recognize the archive office as it is today. In place of the many thousands of dusty boxes containing glass plate negatives and an all-pervading odour of photographic chemicals, there are now ranks of computer screens. He would be amazed to watch his images travelling round the world at unimaginable speeds through network and internet lines.

The archive's future is both bright and exciting. Francis Frith, with his unshakeable belief in making photographs available to the greatest number of people, would undoubtedly approve of what is being done today with his lifetime's work. His photographs, depicting our shared past, are now bringing pleasure and enlightenment to millions around the world a century and more after his death.

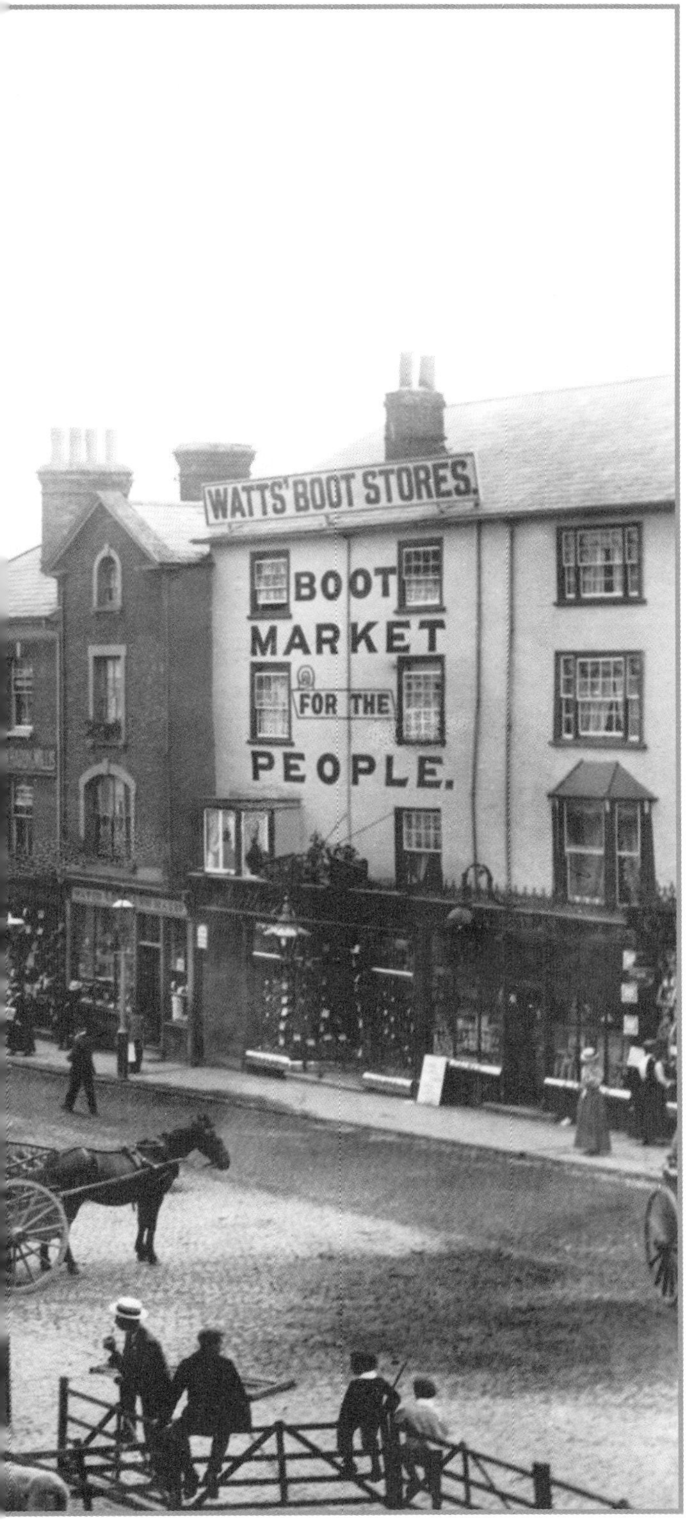

CHAPTER 1

A County of Market and Country Towns

Aylesbury: The County Town

Aylesbury effectively took over from a declining Buckingham as the county town in Henry VIII's reign, when the summer assize courts transferred here to the geographical centre of the county. This ancient hill town prospered in the 18th century, and much of the historic core survived the unfortunate 1960s redevelopment.

Aylesbury, Market Square 1901 47463
Beyond the 1876 clock tower is the pedimented County Hall of the 1720s. Inside is the County Court, and from a scaffold or 'drop' in front of the big arched central window felons were publicly hanged until the 1850s.

FREEMAN, HARDY & WILLIS 27
COACH & HORSES
THE CROSS KEYS
& CO

Aylesbury, Market Square 1901 47461
Looking away from County Hall, the buildings on the left and right disappeared in the 1960s redevelopment while the George Hotel beyond the clock tower was replaced by a modernistic Burton's menswear shop in 1936 - not necessarily an improvement.

◄ **Aylesbury, Market Square, Looking Towards the High Street c1965** A84059
Looking beyond the War Memorial of 1920 is the John Hampden statue. The statue was moved in 1980 nearer to that of Benjamin Disraeli, whose own monument was erected in 1914: they now avoid each other's eye.

◄ **Aylesbury, Market Square 1921** 70552
The livestock market continued in the Market Square until 1927, six years after this view was taken. The railings on the left belong to the statue erected in 1911 of John Hampden, of Ship Money and Civil War fame.

▼ **Aylesbury, Kingsbury Square 1921** 70556
The two pubs remain: The Red Lion on the left, now The Hobgoblin, and the timber-framed The Rockwood, now The Lobster Pot. Beyond the drinking fountain, now in The Vale Park, is the World War I tank displayed here in the 1920s.

◄ **Aylesbury, The Victoria Working Men's Club, Kingsbury 1897** 39627
The imposing (but ugly) Victoria Club was founded for the working men of Aylesbury by Baron Ferdinand Rothschild of Waddesdon in 1897, as one of his many philanthropic works in the county.

Aylesbury, High Street Looking South-East 1897 39625
Longley's, the many-windowed draper's shop on the left, was demolished in 1938 and is now occupied by Marks and Spencers. The early character of the road as houses is still evident in this view.

Aylesbury, High Street 1921 70557
By 1921 commerce has taken over, but few of the buildings shown survive today. The wall on the right belongs to the Congregational Church of 1874, demolished apart from the tower for the Hale Leys Shopping Centre in 1980.

Aylesbury, The Hazell, Watson and Viney Printing Works 1897 39638
This splendidly ornate works and its chimney were an important part of Aylesbury's industrial life from their opening in 1878 to their demolition in the 1980s. The 1850s cemetery has outlived the factory.

Aylesbury, Perambulators Outside the Bell Hotel, Market Square 1921 70563x
This scene outside The Bell Hotel, then a Trust House, shows the brickwork and alterations made to the hotel in 1919. The doorway on the corner has now, perhaps, wisely been changed to a window.

Amersham

Amersham grew up in the valley of the River Misbourne, with steep chalk downs on either side with beech wood crests. It remains remarkably unspoilt, thanks to the care of the Tyrrwhit-Drake family of Shardeloes. Metroland Amersham-on-the-Hill was kept to the heathy plateau, well out of sight, when the railway reached it in 1892.

Amersham, From Parsonage Woods 1958

A148040

Parsonage Woods and the cornfields preserve the open northern setting of the town. This view from the edge of the woods has changed remarkably little, but since 1966 the church has had to compete with an intrusive nurse's home tower block.

Luncheons
Teas
Dinners
The King's Arms
RAC
NOW
BEING
SERVED

Amersham, High Street 1958 A148054
West of the Market Hall, the long High Street has many fine buildings, mostly Georgian brick fronted, but there are also some timber-framed examples such as the celebrated Kings Arms, a 16th-century hall and crosswing house, much enlarged.

Amersham, St Mary's Parish Church 1958 A148069
This view looks over the War Memorial Gardens to the church. The old Weller's Brewery to its right is now converted to housing. To the right of the Memorial Gardens now is the stylish pyramid roofed rectory of 1985.

Amersham, The Church and the Market Square c1955 A148059
In the heart of the town the church and the grand Market Hall are the key buildings. The Hall with its jaunty cupola was built in 1682 by Sir William Drake of Shardeloes, and has miraculously survived highway engineers' traffic safety zeal.

Buckingham:
The Former County Town

The town, on a loop of the River Ouse, was founded by Edward the Elder in 915 AD as a burgh, and became the centre of the county named after it, Buckinghamshire. However, remote at the north-west corner of the county, it declined and lost its county town status to Aylesbury: it has never got over the shock.

Buckingham, The Town Hall and Market Place c1955 B280027
The grand Town Hall, crowned by its gilded swan, closes the south-west side of the Market Square. Rebuilt in 1783, it was already too late - the disastrous fire of 1725 had already ensured Aylesbury's transcendence.

W.H.SMITH & SON
ABDULLA

Buckingham, Market Square 1949 B280004
Not much has changed in this view, apart from the shameful demolition in 1967 of the two-storey building on the right. This was of the 15th century, and decorated with wonderful late 16th-century wall paintings.

Buckingham, Market Hill 1949 B280016
Very few of the buildings survive on the north-west side of the Market Square beyond the white painted part of the King's Head on the right: I wish I could say the 1960s-70s replacements are improvements.

◄ **Buckingham, The Old Gaol c1955** B280028
Built by Lord Cobham of Stowe in 1748 to help regain the assizes for Buckingham, and extended in 1839, the castellated Gothic building has been superbly restored as a fascinating museum. The ivy, of course, has been stripped off.

▼ **Buckingham, High Street c1955** B280015
Further down, into High Street, most buildings survive, with the attractively treed former cattle market on the left, whose trees were originally planted in 1887 as an avenue to the Hospital.

◄ **Buckingham, Bridge Street c1955** B280008
This view looks towards the Market Square from the junction with Well Street. The road curves attractively to the bowed end of the 18th-century Town Hall. The gilded swan now faces to the left.

Buckingham, The River Great Ouse c1955 B280007
Note the the minimal level of children's provision in the 1950s: one swing. It is now much more elaborate with multi-coloured play equipment. This view is from the 1803 London Bridge, erected by the Marquess of Buckingham.

Chesham

Chesham grew up at the junction of streams that feed the River Chess. Noted for its watercress beds, the town also had a number of watermills, and its High Street is partly built over a culverted stream, so tightly constrained was the valley. Other industries included lace-making, paper-making, straw-plaiting and wood-ware, such as malt shovels.

Chesham, The Town Hall 1897 40535
The Town Hall, in the market square originally laid out in the thirteenth century, was rebuilt in 1856 by Lord Chesham. Demolished in 1965 for highway 'improvement', it was replaced by a clock tower in 1992.

GENERAL H. WALLACE IRONMONGER
H. BLOWER

Chesham, High Street 1903 49238
The George and Dragon on the left has its signs still, but the street is now pedestrianised with wall-to-wall herring-bone paviours. The left-hand side buildings were built over a culverted stream, no doubt also serving as a drain.

Chesham, Market Square 1921 70536
The town's 1980s ring-road now passes across the front of this view and the shop on the left made way for it. The square is now mainly pedestrianised and laid out in herring-bone paviours.

Chesham, High Street 1921 70538
By 1921 the 18th-century facade of the George and Dragon looks across the street to the elaborate Queen Anne style National Westminster Bank of about 1912, which replaced two older houses. The old shopfronts have long gone.

Chesham, High Street from the Broadway c1955 C81004
Formerly a hamlet known as Pillory Green, the triangular space was renamed 'The Broadway' and most of its humble cottages were soon replaced. On the left is the old temperance hotel, built when Station Road was laid out around 1892.

Chesham, The Broadway 1897 40533
Looking north out of The Broadway, many of the older cottages still remain. The centre is now occupied by the War Memorial, a soldier with an upturned rifle.

Chesham, The Broadway 1903 49240

Looking towards Blucher Street most of the houses have since gone. Chesham has a long Non-conformist tradition, and their rivalries are reflected in progressively more grandiose church fronts, such as the General Baptist Church of 1902 in this view.

Chesham, Waterside, Looking South from Lord's Mill 1906 53654

Looking south from Lords Mill in Chesham Moor on Waterside little is recognisable now: indeed the mill itself finally went in 1988, although the miller's seventeenth century cottage remains. The ancient mill last ground corn in the 1950s.

Chesham, The Bridge 1921 70546
Looking over the bridge in Germain Street the tree on the right belongs to The Meades, the tanning watermill owner's house. The mill wheel was powered by the River Chess, which was pure enough for cress growing.

JOHN FARMER Ltd
SHIRTS F.H.DRING

High Wycombe

Situated in the narrow valley of the River Wye, this medieval borough developed into a major corn market. The arrival of the furniture industry, based on the 18th-century planting of the Chiltern beech woods, led to considerable Victorian expansion from the Georgian core. Disastrously, the beautiful surrounding hills were carpeted in houses from the 1930s onward.

High Wycombe, The Cornmarket 1951 H84064
The Cornmarket is dominated by the Georgian Guildhall donated to the town by Lord Shelburne in 1757. Retaining its open arcaded ground floor, it closes the vista along the High Street, itself laid out in the thirteenth century as a market.

High Wycombe, The Town in its Valley 1921 70598
This view looking north-west towards the 13th-century parish church from Tom Burt's Hill shows how the town was just beginning to climb out of its narrow river valley through the chalk hills.

High Wycombe, The Town Hall 1906 53663a
Once part of Wycombe Abbey's grounds, the then Lord Carrington donated the land for Queen Victoria Road as a civic precinct in 1901. The orange brick and stone Queen Anne style Town Hall followed in 1904.

High Wycombe, The Technical School in Frogmoor 1906 53671
Frogmoor was once surrounded by prominent citizens' fine Georgian houses, which have now all gone. The 1893 School of Science and Art with its ogee turret became a swimming pool, next The Intimate Theatre and finally in the 1980s offices.

High Wycombe, Frogmoor and the Fountain 1921 70607
Frogmoor, once the western market place of the town, became private gardens which were donated to the town in the 1870s, along with this splendid cast-iron fountain, now long gone and much missed by the citizens.

High Wycombe, Amersham Hill 1906
53668
Amersham Hill, laid out in the late 19th century, replaced a turnpike that climbed the hill further west. Near the railway station, it sprouted large Victorian houses and villas for commuters and Wycombe citizens alike.

Newport Pagnell

Like Buckingham, Newport was an Anglo-Saxon burgh, but acquired its Norman name from the Paynels who founded Tickford Abbey across the River Ouzel. The town's river crossing was of strategic importance, having a castle and its own Civil War siege. Its 18th-century wealth came from the lace industry and, despite modern expansion, retains its market town character.

Newport Pagnell, From the North Bridge over the Great Ouse 1950 N62017
These views capture the town before its 1960s expansion. In fact this view across the flood prone water meadows has changed little, apart from the modernization of the Shell garage on the approaches.

◄ **Newport Pagnell, North Bridge from the Play Pen 1956**

N62050

Children still play and locals picnic by these steps down to the River Great Ouse, set in the former grounds to a fine provincial Baroque house, now the British Legion. Beyond is the graceful stone North Bridge of 1810.

◄ **Newport Pagnell, From the North Bridge Approach Causeway 1956** N62026
Nearer the town, this view is taken just past the 1810 toll house on the north bridge across the River Great Ouse. The house on the right was unfortunately demolished for road improvements in the 1960s.

▼ **Newport Pagnell, The Parish Church from the River Ouzel 1950** N62006
Samuel Pepys described this fine parish church as 'very fair and like a cathedral', mostly 14th century with a 16th-century tower that dominates the townscape, its south side faces the River Ouzel in an almost rural setting.

◄ **Newport Pagnell, High Street 1956** N62023
Further west the High Street widens out to the site of its medieval market place. This view from beside The Dolphin pub shows how important the Tudor church tower is to the townscape.

HAIRDRESSER
TOBACCONIST.
TAILOR
CAFE
CAFE

Newport Pagnell, High Street 1956
N62052
Although some buildings have been replaced since 1956, this view retains the market town character that led John Betjeman to describe the town in 1948 as 'a small midland country town with dark brick Georgian houses, tall Victorian shopfronts'.

Newport Pagnell, The Coachmakers Arms 1955 N62038
Despite its rural feel, the Coachmakers Arms is in the town behind the former Town Hall (actually built as a school and now a Baptist church), and St Bede's Roman Catholic Church which was originally built as the police station.

Newport Pagnell, St John Street 1950 N62015
Tragically the left hand side of the road was demolished in the 1960s and replaced by appaling flat-roofed buildings. The road descends to the elegant 1810 cast-iron Tickford Bridge: the oldest surviving still in regular vehicular use.

Stony Stratford

Now swallowed up in the new town/city of Milton Keynes, the town struggles fairly successfully to keep its identity. Situated on Roman Watling Street at its crossing of the River Great Ouse, the long High Street has many fine brick and stone buildings, while the 13th-century market place was laid out south-west of High Street.

Stony Stratford, High Street 1906 S266001
Looking north along High Street, remarkably little has changed. The low building on the right was apparently the site of the medieval George Inn, where in 1483 Richard III captured Edward, later murdered in the Tower of London.

The
TWO
BREWERS
THE
WHITE
SWAN
INN.

Wendover

Wendover, a small market town, grew up where a valley route emerges from the Chiltern Hills. Great things were expected for the town when the Wendover Arm of the Grand Junction Canal was opened in 1797, but it leaked and was a failure. The Metropolitan Railway arrived in 1892 and the town at last expanded.

Wendover, High Street, Looking North-East 1901 47472
The High Street is seen here descending past the White Swan to the Clock Tower, given to the town in 1842 as a miniature market hall and lock-up. The clock tower part arrived in 1870.

Wendover, Pound Street 1901 47471
This view is from by the station approach and is little changed, although the pavements and road are more formalised. The Shoulder of Mutton clearly wished to attract railway passengers and added 'or Station Hotel' to its name.

Wendover, Coldharbour Cottages, Tring Road 1899 44771
This wonderful range of 17th-century thatched timber-framed cottages sweeps down the Tring Road towards the clock tower. Unfortunately, since then, the road has been considerably widened and the walls moved about 60 ft further away as concrete retaining walls.

CHAPTER 2:
Temples of Delight: Some Buckinghamshire Country Houses

Stowe

Stowe is of European importance in the history of landscape gardening. Its 18th-century picturesque naturalistic park, designed by Bridgeman, Kent and Capability Brown, is dotted with Georgian temples, columns and garden buildings. After its decline in the nineteenth century, Stowe School was founded in 1923 and the grounds are now owned by The National Trust.

Stowe, The Rotondo and the School's Chatham House c1960 B280062
The School buildings, seen from across Eleven Acre Lake, were intended to fit into the Georgian parkland. Designed in 1924 by Clough Williams-Ellis, the architect of Portmeirion, they compete with Vanbrugh's 1721 Rotondo temple on the right.

▼ **Stowe, The School's Chapel Court c1960** B280053
Sir John Vanbrugh's 1718 Orangery on the right, muscular arcades and a pedimented two-storey centre, rather shows up Clough Williams-Ellis' classroom block on the left. At the right is a service wing of Lord Cobham's great Georgian mansion.

▼ **Stowe, The Queen's Temple 1967** B280105
Originally the Lady's Temple (for Lady Cobham's use), it was built in 1743 by James Gibbs, altered in the 1770s and is now a music room for the school. It looks down the valley to the men's Temple of Friendship.

▲ **Stowe, The Palladian Bridge c1960** B280068
Copied by James Gibbs from the one at Wilton House in Wiltshire, this bridge from 1738 crosses the end of the Octagon Lake. It is based on a design by the great century Italian architect, Andrea Palladio.

◄ **Stowe, The Corinthian Arch c1955** B280032
The Corinthian Arch terminates Lord Cobham's mile long avenue from Buckingham, bought and saved by Clough Williams-Ellis. Through the centre of the giant archway of 1765 Stowe mansion facade is seen a mile away.

Hedsor

Wonderfully situated on open hillside above the Thames, the medieval manor house was rebuilt by Rowland Hynd in 1583. Little remains except the garden walls east of the church for the main mansion, Hedsor House, which was rebuilt further uphill to the south for Lord Boston. Much of its 18th-century parkland remains intact.

Hedsor Park, The Parish Church and Lord Boston's Folly 1890 23655
St Nicholas's Church, amid rolling parkland in its hedged churchyard, looks across to the 18th century battlemented towers of Lord Boston's Folly, a romantic hilltop eyecatcher in the form of a castle, now converted to a house.

Wycombe Abbey

Originally Loakes Manor, a 17th-century manor house in grounds laid out by Capability Brown, the house was remodelled by James Wyatt in 1803 for the then Lord Carrington, acquiring the romantic Wycombe Abbey name. In 1896 his lordship moved up the hill to Daws Hill House and the Abbey became a pioneering girls' public school.

Left: **Wycombe Abbey, The East Front 1906** 53688
Wyatt clad the brick house in the local hard granite-like Denner Hill Stone and gothicised the house with turrets and battlements. In this view the creeper clad house has been a school for ten years.

Below: **Wycombe Abbey, The Rupert Lodge and Gates 1906** 53679
Originally built as the entrance to Wycombe Abbey's grounds from the High Street, the lodge and gateway were relocated by Lord Carrington in 1891 halfway up Marlow Hill for his Daws Hill House.

Stoke Park
Stoke Poges

You could be forgiven for thinking Stoke Park looks vaguely like Washington's White House, for there is an American connection. John Penn, who built the mansion in 1789 upon his return from America, was the grandson of William Penn, who had founded the State of Pennsylvania in 1683.

Stoke Park, The North Front 1895 35463
Set in parkland laid out by Capability Brown and Humphrey Repton, and now a golf course, the stucco mansion by Nasmith, was much improved and enlarged in the 1790s by James Wyatt who also added the dome.

Waddesdon Manor

Baron Ferdinand de Rothschild bought the estate in 1874, and transformed a bare hill-top west of Aylesbury into a wooded park crowned by the spectacular French chateau we see today, while Waddesdon village became an estate village. Ferdinand was one of the Rothschilds who made their homes at Aston Clinton, Mentmore, Eythrope, Halton and Ascott, which transformed Victorian Buckinghamshire.

Waddesdon Manor, The Lake 1897 39661
An extraordinary view: for instead of the great chateau by the French architect, Destailleur, Frith's photographer chose to photograph the lake down by the home farm whose granary can be see out on the right.

Waddesdon Manor, The Rothschild Village 1901 47469
Down in the village, Rothschild built The Five Arrows Hotel in 1887 for visitors, a splendid Arts and Crafts building with elaborate moulded brick chimneys. The five arrows was the badge of the five Rothschild brothers.

Waddesdon Manor, The Rothschild Village, High Street 1901 47470
Other Rothschild improvements included rebuilding the 17th-century almshouses seen on the left in 1893 and, beyond, providing a stylish village Hall in 1897. There was a village here before and it has a fine medieval parish church.

CHAPTER 3

Village Buckinghamshire

Burnham

Burnham desperately struggles to keep its identity separate from the sprawl of Slough, but the historic core is surrounded by suburban housing. To the south of the Bath Road or the A4, in the flat fields west of Slough, lies Burnham Abbey with substantial remains of a medieval nunnery, and since 1916 an Anglican nunnery.

Burnham, High Street c1955 B250010
In 1955 the long winding High Street survived more or less intact. On the right all buildings up to and including the tree have gone: instead there is now a supermarket building.

Farnham Royal
and Farnham Common

The Farnhams straggle north along the A355 Beaconsfield Road. Farnham Royal (the 'royal' referring to William the Conqueror granting to the lord of the manor the right to provide a glove for his coronation), focuses on the crossroads with the Burnham and Stoke Poges roads with the partly medieval church nearby.

Farnham Royal, The Village Centre, Looking North c1955 F195040
The village pump with its steep octagonal roof donated in 1928 to replace the original has now been relocated 50 yards further west to make way for roundabouts. The shop building on the right has now gone.

Farnham Royal, The Village Centre, Looking East c1955 F195009
The Jolly Butcher pub is now called The Farnham Pump, in honour of the relocated pump house, but the cedar trees and the houses along the north side of Park Road remain virtually unchanged.

Farnham Common, The Victoria Hotel c1965 F196024
In Victoria Road, just east of the A355 as it passes through Farnham Common, the late 19th-century Victoria Hotel is now The Victoria, with its brickwork painted cream and the window jambs and quoins dark blue.

Gawcott

Gawcott, the scene of a great agricultural labourers strike in 1867, was the birthplace of George Gilbert Scott, the architect of St Pancras Station, the Albert Memorial and the Foreign Office, besides countless churches. Born in 1811, his father, Thomas, designed the Classical style parish church of 1827. Did his sixteen-year-old son help, one wonders?

Gawcott, The Village c1955 G229011
Since the 1950s, the thatched cottage has gone, to be replaced by executive houses, but The Crown pub still quenches the village thirst. The Jubilee telephone kiosk has been removed, but unfortunately the overhead electricity cables remain.

Haddenham

Haddenham is renowned for its earth walled buildings and boundary walls, known locally as 'witchert' or white earth and Buckinghamshire's version of cob. Based on the local lime rich sub-soil it produces high quality walls that, if protected by a low foundation wall and a good roof, can last hundreds of years.

Haddenham, St Mary's Church c1955 H357031
At Church End the serene arcaded 13th-century church tower looks over the duck pond out of view to the left. Duck rearing was a somewhat odoriferous staple for the village in the 18th century.

Haddenham, Church End Green c1955

H375006

Looking beyond the war memorial on the west side of Church End Green, this view captures the character of this long village. Two of the houses were once pubs and the sash windowed one on the right a maltster's house.

NORTHAMPTON

Lavendon

Lavendon, Buckinghamshire's northernmost village, is in the limestone belt with its houses mostly stone-built. Dominated by its fine church, which is substantially Anglo-Saxon with later aisles and tower top, the village achieved national fame when the Jarrow Hunger Marchers came through in 1936 and were fed, watered and rested by sympathetic villagers.

Left: **Lavendon, High Street 1952** L201007
The village, on the Northampton to Bedford road, is now plagued by heavy traffic. On the left is the church yard wall while the shop on the right, now a house, retains its Royal Mail letter box.

Below: **Lavendon, The Post Office and Square c1965** L201025
The post office has moved into the shop beyond, and in the distance is the Union Chapel of 1894. On the right, The George Inn is now a private house, renamed, unsurprisingly, The Old George House.

Maids Moreton

The 'maids' in the village name were the unmarried Peover sisters who endowed and rebuilt the superb Perpendicular parish church around 1450. It is a curious village with large numbers of small 17th- and 18th-century cottages, many in very flimsy timber-framing, contrasting with two or three grand Victorian houses

Maids Moreton, The Village c1955 M264006
The thatched Chestnut Cottage on the left is a good example of the scanty late timber-framing characteristic of the village cottages. Beyond are 19th-century cottages with the village shop and post office still functioning.

Maids Moreton, The Village c1955 M264008
All three thatched roofs remain at the south end of Main Street. Holly Tree Cottage on the right now has its 17th-century timber-framing exposed while beyond are the grounds of The Red House, a Victorian mansion which is now a nursing home.

Maids Moreton, The Leys c1955 M264012
North of Main Street, the dignified 1950s council housing was built on The Leys field. In the foreground Old Page's Cottage is another of Maids Moreton's late timber-framed cottages, with thin timbers and a thatched roof.

Oving

Situated on a Portland limestone ridge with superb long views over the clay Vale of Aylesbury, Oving has a mixture of limestone, timber-framed and brick houses and cottages. The bulk of the old village is off the through road, and thus retains a tranquillity that nearby Whitchurch totally lacks.

Oving, The Village c1955 O118006
Magpie Cottage on the left is a fine 17th-century timber-framed building, presumably named because of the black and white of the timbers and the rendered panelling. Note the friable Portland limestone in other walls.

Oving, The Black Boy Inn c1955 O118004
This 17th-century timber-framed inn, with its picturesque jumble of old tiled roofs is still very popular for the superb views north from the ridge across the vale towards Buckingham, quite apart from its good food.

Oving, Manor Road c1955 O118008
Looking north along this lane which leads to the main street, Tinker End Cottages on the right are a fine group of 18th- and 19th-century labourers' cottages. The distant chimney is that of The Manor House.

Stokenchurch

Until 1896, Stokenchurch was within the parish of Aston Rowant in Oxfordshire when it was transferred, with parts of Ibstone to Buckinghamshire. It is grouped around three large greens and has a good medieval church at its north end, a spectacularly quirky methodist church of 1893 and is bisected east to west by the A40.

▼ **Stokenchurch, The Common c1955** S685034
Looking across Bowling Green to the south side of Oxford Road, these houses are mainly early and later 19th century. The modest petrol station has now expanded and the houses on each side of the Esso sign have now gone.

▲ **Stokenchurch, The Oxford Road c1955**
S685018
The telegraph wires have long gone to be succeeded by other media, and although most of the houses in this view remain, the place is virtually unrecognisable and the traffic scanty: this is the main A40 London to Oxford road.

◄ **Stokenchurch, The Water Tower c1955** S685036
Water had always been a problem on this dry plateau, and the centre of the village was disfigured until a few years ago by this 1930s concrete water tower: like a parody church.

Stoke Poges

East of Stoke Park, the medieval church of Stoke Poges is famous beyond its architecture: this is reputedly the churchyard of Thomas Gray's, 'Elegy from a Country Churchyard', one of the most well known and loved of all English poems. From the churchyard itself you can see the tall Gray Monument erected by John Penn of Stoke Park in 1799.

Left: **Stoke Poges, St Giles' Church 1895** 35457
The spire, a timber one added in 1702, was replaced by the present low tiled pyramid in 1924, for the visual benefit of the church. The creeper has now gone, exposing the Tudor brick of the Hastings Chapel on the left.

Below: **Stoke Poges, Church Cottage 1929** 82277
This rustic assemblage remains south-east of the church, and east of the delightful Memorial Gardens which are open to the public. The cottage was restored after the photograph was taken and the dormer and many windows replaced.

Taplow

Taplow village runs east-west where the chalk hills drop down towards the valley of the River Thames. Taplow Court, now a Tudor-Gothic 1840s mansion in superb grounds, is at the west end. The original parish church, demolished in 1828, used to be near the house, but was rebuilt at the east end of the village.

Taplow, The Village 1906 54109
Soon after this view was taken, looking south at the start of Berry Hill's steep descent towards the A4 Bath Road, the thatched cottage was replaced by a larger Arts & Crafts version by the Taplow Estate.

West Wycombe

West Wycombe is probably the finest, least altered historic village in the county. Bought from the Dashwoods by the Royal Society of Arts in 1929, it was given to The National Trust in 1934. West Wycombe Hill was given in 1933, and the wonderful West Wycombe Park House and landscaped park came to the Trust in 1943.

West Wycombe, The High Street, Looking West 1906 53690
Not a building out of place: it is remarkable that the village survived intact, despite being on the main London to Oxford road until the M40 was opened. Timber-frames, and Georgian brick blend into a superbly picturesque combination.

Whiteleaf

Whiteleaf, a corruption of 'white cliff', is a delightful hamlet straggling along the Upper Icknield Way, a Neolithic trackway from Avebury in Wiltshire to Thetford in Norfolk. It lies below the famous Whiteleaf Cross, cut into the chalk of the Chiltern scarp face, and was a hamlet in the ancient parish of Monks Risborough.

Left: **Whiteleaf, Cottages in the Village c1955** P282013
A couple of years after this view of 17th-century thatched cottages at the east end of the village was taken, the cottage on the right burnt down and was rebuilt in brick with a tiled roof.

Below: **Whiteleaf, Cottages c1955** P282061
At the west end of the village is a fine group of cottages, the timber-framed ones 16th century, and the thatched one with flint walls 18th century. On the left, the thatched cottage, Library Cottage, has recently been rebuilt.

Wooburn Green

Wooburn Green, in the valley of the River Wye, has a delightful green and, to the south, the site of a moated palace of the medieval bishops of Lincoln. Later in the early 18th century the Duke of Wharton created a vast mansion from the palace. Tragically the remnants were demolished in 1964 and replaced by a housing estate.

Wooburn Green, The Green, Looking North-East 1910 62236
This view shows the south corner of The Green, nowadays more defined by mature trees along its perimeter. Ten years later the War Memorial replaced the signpost: a mute testament to the lost men of the village.

Wooburn Town

Although the medieval manor house of the D'Eyncourt family was demolished in the 1920s for road widening, the fine parish church remains. To the west is the River Wye and the site of Soho Mills, huge paper mills, much expanded from the original watermill, that until recently overwhelmed the village.

Wooburn Town, The village, Looking South-West 1910 62231
These nineteenth century facades fronted older buildings. No longer shops, they have been decked out with modern leaded casements and bow windows. To the right behind the tree (now gone) is the wall to the churchyard.

CHAPTER 4

Buckinghamshire: Wood and Water

Aylesbury

The Grand Junction Canal, now The Grand Union, was built between 1793 and 1805 to link Birmingham with the River Thames and London. Numerous branch canals were constructed to it, including the Aylesbury Branch which finally opened in 1815. An immediate consequence was the halving of coal prices in Aylesbury!

The Aylesbury Arm of the Grand Union Canal 1921 70564
Looking north from Park Street Lock, whose gate mechanisms are dated 1855 and 1862, the buildings have disappeared, but canal boats still moor here. Admittedly they are now mostly houseboats, the industrial traffic having long disappeared.

Bourne End

The River Thames enjoyed a Victorian and Edwardian boating boom, enjoyed by all classes of society, captured by Marlow resident Jerome K. Jerome's celebrated boating novel 'Three Men In A Boat'. On Saturdays, Sundays and holidays the river seethed with rowing boats, steam launches and sailing boats, wonderfully depicted by another Marlow resident E. J. Gregory's famous painting Boulter's Lock.

Bourne End, Boats on the River Thames 1899 43959
This late Victorian scene records a relatively quiet moment on a summer afternoon. In the distance is the railway bridge of the Maidenhead to Wycombe railway line, the branch line to Marlow opening in 1873.

Bourne End, The Marina and Boat Yard from the Berkshire Bank 1899 43963
Townsend's and Shaw's boatyards and their wharfs were a focus of boating activity and the renowned annual Bourne End Regatta was based there, established in 1897. Later, besides boat building and repairing, a marina developed.

Burnham Beeches

A Victorian naturalist, amazingly named Heath, suggested that the Corporation of London should buy these ancient woodlands and scrub, full of majestic but neglected ancient pollarded beech trees. Eventually in 1880 they bought about 80 hectares for the enjoyment of all and, like their purchase of Epping Forest, for Londoners.

Burnham Beeches 1929 81697
The beeches were in a poor state by 1880, having not been pollarded for over sixty years. These beautiful 17th-century beech trees had been regularly pollarded for fuel for London until supplanted by coal.

Denham

The Grand Union Canal plays an important role in the Buckinghamshire landscape as it heads south from Birmingham to Brentford. Starting in the 1790s with vigorous support from Buckinghamshire's nobility, gentry and traders, it took until March 1805 for it to open fully. The canal is mainly used for leisure purposes now, but who knows what cargoes the future may bring?

Denham, The Grand Union Canal Lock, Moorfield Road c1965 D183005
Widewater Lock with its early 19th-century hipped slate roofed lock keeper's cottage and lock with gate mechanisms dated 1876, is typical of the architecture all along the canal. Nearby is a former bargee's pub, the Horse and Barge.

Denham, The Boat Yard, Moorfield Road c1965 D183002
Opposite the Horse and Barge pub is what is now named The Harefield Marina, a basin with a typical selection of pleasure craft, from long canal boats for holidays or living to motor boats, the latter nowadays much posher.

Dorney

The Countryside Commission's recently opened Thames Path, a long distance footpath which follows much of the River Thames on the Buckinghamshire bank along the old barge towing paths. Until the railways took most of the trade, the river was the cheapest and most efficient method of transporting bulk goods, such as coal, building materials and corn.

Dorney, The Reach 1951 D87007
Since 1951 this tranquil stretch of the towing path has had its peace shattered: now in the middle distance an elegant duck egg blue painted steel bridge carries the ceaseless roar of the M4's traffic.

Hambleden

The River Thames has always been a busy river, used mainly for trade and commerce. Its weirs were provided with by-pass locks, nowadays gated at each end. Until the late 18th century they were single gated flashlocks, through which the barges and boats were perilously swept or 'flashed' downstream and then hauled upstream by ropes and capstans.

Hambleden, The Lock 1890 27217
Since 1773, Hambleden Lock has been a pound or two gated lock, but this view has changed completely. The lock-keeper's house was rebuilt in 1928, and the lock completely rebuilt and widened in 1993.

Hedsor

Among the great improvements made after 1770 by the River Thames' Commissioners was the elimination of flashlocks and their replacement with safer pound or double gated locks. Cookham Lock is one of these located at the south end of a cut, made to by-pass the river's wide loop below Hedsor with its two weirs.

Hesdor, The Weir 1890 23659
Hedsor Weir is the second weir in the Hedsor loop, the first being immediately east of Cookham Bridge where the canal cut starts. Tucked in close to the river cliff, the weir is seen from the south.

High Wycombe

The River Wye, flowing from West Wycombe to the River Thames at Bourne End, powered about thirty watermills. Mainly paper making mills, but a few were flour mills and there was the odd fulling mill. Several of them survive in varying states of completeness, and are a vital part of the county's industrial heritage.

High Wycombe, Marsh Green Mill 1906 53674
Marsh Green Mill, also known as Darvill's Mill, was an important paper mill. Burnt down during the 1830s machine-breaking riots and then rebuilt. Its pond is now filled in and the mill converted to houses.

High Wycombe, The Beeches 1921 70608
This view in the beech woods above High Wycombe, is a reminder of the town's great chair and furniture industry, based on 'bodgers' turning chair legs and components in the woods for finishing and assembly in the town.

Marlow

This delightful riverside town, not as well-known perhaps as Henley, with the Chilterns hemming it in to the north, has fine Georgian streets and early 19th-century houses. Its Georgian mansions include Marlow Place, and Remnantz, the first home of the Royal Military Academy before it moved to Sandhurst in 1812.

Left: **Marlow, From the Lock 1890** 23672
From the east, by the lock by-passing Marlow Weir, the earlier spire of the parish church was a peculiarly knobbly one with giant crockets. The Dutch gabled Bridge House on the right dates from 1860.

Below: **Marlow, The Bridge and the Parish Church from the West 1893** 31738
The parish church of All Saints replaced the medieval one pulled down in 1830, and was in an incorrect early Gothic revival style. The spire in this view was replaced in 1899 by today's graceful one.

Marlow, Fisherman's Retreat 1890 23690
St Peter Street had several rows of cottages, some in great dilapidation, occupied by river workers such as ferrymen, bargees and wharfingers. Those on the left have been replaced by the Neo-Georgian complex of Fisherman's Retreat.

◄ **Marlow, The Boat Yard 1890** 23681
Looking down from the suspension bridge, the boatyard seems a low key affair. The boats then, as now, were pleasure craft. The two houses on the right survive, but are altered and flanked by modern blocks of flats.

▼ **Marlow, The Weir 1901** 47129
This view, below the weir, shows the church with its more refined spire. Newly completed, it was designed by John Oldrid Scott, second son of George Gilbert Scott, the great Victorian architect born in Gawcott, near Buckingham.

◄ **Marlow, From the Lock 1901** 47125
Tranquil summer boating on the Thames: a rowing boat approaches the lock. The three people in the boat remind one of Jerome K. Jerome's 'Three Men in a Boat' who lived near this part of the river in Marlow.

Taplow

North of Maidenhead, the River Thames cuts in close on the Buckinghamshire bank to the beautiful tree-clad chalk river cliffs that rise 150 ft to the chalk plateau. Several country houses and their grounds took full advantage of the long views this lofty position gave: Taplow Court, Cliveden and Hedsor House.

Taplow, The River Thames 1890 23638
Looking from the Berkshire bank across the Cliveden Deep, the 1850s estate cottages and boathouse of the Cliveden Estate are hidden by trees beyond the boats. The towpath bank is now tree-lined unfortunately and this view is only glimpsed.

Whiteleaf

The Chiltern Hills, now a designated Area of Outstanding Natural Beauty, are a chalk range of hills with a north-west facing escarpment that crosses Buckinghamshire from Stokenchurch to Ivinghoe, their highest point is in Wendover Woods at over 850 ft. They are more wooded than the South Downs, for example, with large acreages of beech wood: leafy Bucks.

Whiteleaf Cross and The Chilterns 1897 39644
The Whiteleaf and Bledlow Crosses are Buckinghamshire's only significant chalk-cut features on the Chiltern escarpment. Whiteleaf Cross, its lower part now obscured by trees, was first mentioned in 1742 but its origins are obscure, although some think it Anglo-Saxon.

CHAPTER 5

Metroland and Modern Bucks

Beaconsfield: Old and New

The historic town of Beaconsfield with its four main streets called Ends: Wycombe, Windsor, Aylesbury and London, is nowadays known as The Old Town. It is the far south-east corner of a huge rectangle of 20th-century development, Beaconsfield New Town with its railway station for London commuters.

▼ **Beaconsfield, The Old Town c1955** B609018
Looking across from the war memorial in Windsor End, this view shows the range of fine historic buildings, with Georgian and early 19th-century refrontings to earlier Tudor buildings that so characterise the old town.

▲ **Beaconsfield, The New Town c1960** B609078
There are many fine houses in the generously laid out leafy suburban roads of the New Town. In its shopping centre the Neo-Georgian block on the left contrasts with the half-timbering of Burkes Parade, but all good quality work of the 1920s.

◄ Beaconsfield, Bekonskot Model Village c1955

B609066

Bekonskot is one of the most famous model villages and is still popular. Though a little dated now it has a quaint charm in this hi-tec age. It was started in 1929 as a hobby by Roland Callingham

Bletchley

Now within Milton Keynes's city boundaries, Bletchley grew from a small village with the arrival of the railway, then the brickworks and other industry, and boomed as a London Overspill town in the 1950s. Thus, it has a great mix of Victorian and later housing. It cannot be called a beautiful town.

Bletchley, Victoria Road c1955 B439025
Victoria Road is, unsurprisingly, typical of the mid to late Victorian development of the town with terraces of two storey houses and small shops. In the distance is the former Stony Stratford Board School of 1890.

Bletchley, Queensway Shopping Parade c1965 B439056
Archetypal 1960s Bletchley, these shopping parades were provided for the London Overspill expansion of the town. This section is now pedestrianised, albeit using poor quality materials, and the centrepiece of the parade, Woolworths, has gone.

Bletchley Park c1965 B439070
Architecturally something of a dog's dinner with bits added to the 1860 house piecemeal, Bletchley Park is famous for the cracking of the Nazi 'Enigma' code during the last war, admittedly in huts around the site.

Bourne End

Bourne End owes its development mainly to the arrival of the Maidenhead to High Wycombe railway line in 1854, a branch from the Great Western main line. There is a fair amount of Victorian development, but the real expansion came this century, and included the Abbotsbrook Estate, an Edwardian garden suburb of great character.

Bourne End, The Parade c1960 B160034
By 1955 Bourne End Parade was mostly rebuilt. The 1890s shops on the left belong to its first phase, and the then new parades opposite were the height of fashion. The garage has been totally rebuilt since.

Denham

The Grand Union Canal plays an important role in the Buckinghamshire landscape as it heads south from Birmingham to Brentford. Begun in the 1790s with vigorous support from the county's nobility, gentry and traders, it took until March 1805 for it to open fully. The canal is used mainly for leisure purposes now, but who knows what the future may bring?

Denham, The Main Street, Looking South-East c1965 D183020
The village street runs north-west from the church towards Denham Place, a splendid country house in walled grounds of 1688-1701, then turns south-west and over the River Misbourne: all remarkably peaceful so close to the M25 and M40.

Farnham Common

The Farnhams have some pre-20th century buildings: not surprisingly, as they lie along the road from Windsor to Beaconsfield and Amersham. However, their greatest expansion undoubtedly came this century. Not quite Metroland, of course, but rural suburban and well away from Slough. They also are flanked by the beautiful Burnham Beeches and Farnham Common.

Farnham Common, The Parade c1965 F196006
This suburban shopping street, with some 19th-century buildings, is dominated by the 1950s shopping parade, like a refugee from Beaconsfield New Town. For some reason The Stag and Hounds has since been rebuilt.

Princes Risborough

Princes Risborough is a fine market town that owes its name to the Black Prince, the victor of Crecy, who held the manor in the 14th century and had his royal stud farm here. The town has a medieval church and market hall, as well as many good period houses.

Princes Risborough, The Catholic Church of St Teresa of Avila c1955 P282006
On the east side of town, the Roman Catholic church of St Teresa is an extraordinary brick building with a hexagonal dome and six apses. It was designed by the Italian, Giuseppe Rinvolucri in 1938.

Woburn Sands

A curiously amorphous settlement on the Bedfordshire border, the town developed when the Bedford Branch railway arrived in 1846, with its Bedford Estate style half-timbered station. Suburban villas line the road uphill from the station to the village/town centre, at the crossroads of the Newport Pagnell and Bedford roads.

Woburn Sands, High Street c1955 W434023
The war memorial at the distant crossroads has been relocated near to The Institute of 1874, while The Swan is now clad in painted weatherboarding. Beyond, are the trees that cover the Greensand hills of Apsley Heath in Bedfordshire.

Index

FRITH BOOK Co

Frith Book Co Titles

Frith Book Company publish over 100 new titles each year. For latest catalogue please contact Frith Book Co.

Town Books 96pp, 100 photos. County and Themed Books 128pp, 150 photos (unless specified) All titles hardback laminated case and jacket except those indicated pb (paperback)

Around Bakewell	1-85937-113-2	£12.99
Around Barnstaple	1-85937-084-5	£12.99
Around Bath	1-85937-097-7	£12.99
Around Blackpool	1-85937-049-7	£12.99
Around Bognor Regis	1-85937-055-1	£12.99
Around Bournemouth	1-85937-067-5	£12.99
Around Bristol	1-85937-050-0	£12.99
British Life A Century Ago	1-85937-103-5	£17.99
Around Cambridge	1-85937-092-6	£12.99
Cambridgeshire	1-85937-086-1	£14.99
Cheshire	1-85937-045-4	£14.99
Around Chester	1-85937-090-X	£12.99
Around Chesterfield	1-85937-071-3	£12.99
Around Chichester	1-85937-089-6	£12.99
Cornwall	1-85937-054-3	£14.99
Cotswolds	1-85937-099-3	£14.99
Cumbria	1-85937-101-9	£14.99
Around Derby	1-85937-046-2	£12.99
Devon	1-85937-052-7	£14.99
Dorset	1-85937-075-6	£14.99
Dorset Coast	1-85937-062-4	£14.99
Down the Thames	1-85937-121-3	£14.99
Around Dublin	1-85937-058-6	£12.99
East Anglia	1-85937-059-4	£14.99
Around Eastbourne	1-85937-061-6	£12.99
English Castles	1-85937-078-0	£14.99
Essex	1-85937-082-9	£14.99
Around Exeter	1-85937-126-4	£12.99
Around Falmouth	1-85937-066-7	£12.99
Around Great Yarmouth	1-85937-085-3	£12.99
Greater Manchester	1-85937-108-6	£14.99
Hampshire	1-85937-064-0	£14.99
Around Harrogate	1-85937-112-4	£12.99
Hertfordshire	1-85937-079-9	£14.99
Isle of Man	1-85937-065-9	£14.99
Isle of Wight	1-85937-114-0	£14.99
Around Leicester	1-85937-073-x	£12.99
Around Lincoln	1-85937-111-6	£12.99
Around Liverpool	1-85937-051-9	£12.99
Around Maidstone	1-85937-056-X	£12.99
North Yorkshire	1-85937-048-9	£14.99
Northumberland and Tyne & Wear	1-85937-072-1	£14.99
Around Nottingham	1-85937-060-8	£12.99
Around Oxford	1-85937-096-9	£12.99
Oxfordshire	1-85937-076-4	£14.99
Around Penzance	1-85937-069-1	£12.99
Around Plymouth	1-85937-119-1	£12.99
Around Reading	1-85937-087-X	£12.99
Around St Ives	1-85937-068-3	£12.99
Around Salisbury	1-85937-091-8	£12.99
Around Scarborough	1-85937-104-3	£12.99
Scottish Castles	1-85937-077-2	£14.99
Around Sevenoaks and Tonbridge	1-85937-057-8	£12.99
Sheffield and S Yorkshire	1-85937-070-5	£14.99
Around Southport	1-85937-106-x	£12.99
Around Shrewsbury	1-85937-110-8	£12.99
Shropshire	1-85937-083-7	£14.99
South Devon Coast	1-85937-107-8	£14.99
Staffordshire (96pp)	1-85937-047-0	£12.99
Around Stratford upon Avon	1-85937-098-5	£12.99
Suffolk	1-85937-074-8	£14.99
Surrey	1-85937-081-0	£14.99
Around Torbay	1-85937-063-2	£12.99
Welsh Castles	1-85937-120-5	£14.99
West Midlands	1-85937-109-4	£14.99
Wiltshire	1-85937-053-5	£14.99

Frith Book Co Titles Available in 2000

Canals and Waterways	1-85937-129-9	£17.99	Apr
Around Guildford	1-85937-117-5	£12.99	Apr
Around Horsham	1-85937-127-2	£12.99	Apr
Around Ipswich	1-85937-133-7	£12.99	Apr
Ireland (pb)	1-85937-181-7	£9.99	Apr
London (pb)	1-85937-183-3	£9.99	Apr
New Forest	1-85937-128-0	£14.99	Apr
Around Newark	1-85937-105-1	£12.99	Apr
Around Newquay	1-85937-140-x	£12.99	Apr
Scotland (pb)	1-85937-182-5	£9.99	Apr
Around Southampton	1-85937-088-8	£12.99	Apr
Sussex (pb)	1-85937-184-1	£9.99	Apr
Around Winchester	1-85937-139-6	£12.99	Apr

Around Belfast	1-85937-094-2	£12.99	May
Colchester (pb)	1-85937-188-4	£8.99	May
Dartmoor	1-85937-145-0	£14.99	May
Exmoor	1-85937-132-9	£14.99	May
Leicestershire (pb)	1-85937-185-x	£9.99	May
Lincolnshire	1-85937-135-3	£14.99	May
North Devon Coast	1-85937-146-9	£14.99	May
Nottinghamshire (pb)	1-85937-187-6	£9.99	May
Peak District	1-85937-100-0	£14.99	May
Redhill to Reigate	1-85937-137-x	£12.99	May
Around Truro	1-85937-147-7	£12.99	May
Yorkshire (pb)	1-85937-186-8	£9.99	May

Berkshire (pb)	1-85937-191-4	£9.99	Jun
Brighton (pb)	1-85937-192-2	£8.99	Jun
Churches of Berkshire	1-85937-170-1	£17.99	Jun
Churches of Dorset	1-85937-172-8	£17.99	Jun
Derbyshire (pb)	1-85937-196-5	£9.99	Jun
East Sussex	1-85937-130-2	£14.99	Jun
Edinburgh (pb)	1-85937-193-0	£8.99	Jun
Norwich (pb)	1-85937-194-9	£8.99	Jun
South Devon Living Memories	1-85937-168-x	£14.99	Jun
Stone Circles & Ancient Monuments	1-85937-143-4	£17.99	Jun
Victorian & Edwardian Kent	1-85937-149-3	£14.99	Jun
Warwickshire (pb)	1-85937-203-1	£9.99	Jun

Buckinghamshire (pb)	1-85937-200-7	£9.99	Jul
Down the Severn	1-85937-118-3	£14.99	Jul
Kent (pb)	1-85937-189-2	£9.99	Jul
Victorian & Edwardian Yorkshire	1-85937-154-x	£14.99	Jul
West Sussex	1-85937-148-5	£14.99	Jul

Cornish Coast	1-85937-163-9	£14.99	Aug
County Durham	1-85937-123-x	£14.99	Aug
Croydon Living Memories	1-85937-162-0	£12.99	Aug
Dorsert Living Memories	1-85937-210-4	£14.99	Aug
Glasgow (pb)	1-85937-190-6	£8.99	Aug
Gloucestershire	1-85937-102-7	£14.99	Aug
Herefordshire	1-85937-174-4	£14.99	Aug
Kent Living Memories	1-85937-125-6	£14.99	Aug
Lancashire (pb)	1-85937-197-3	£9.99	Aug
Manchester (pb)	1-85937-198-1	£8.99	Aug
North London	1-85937-206-6	£14.99	Aug
Somerset	1-85937-153-1	£14.99	Aug
Tees Valley & Cleveland	1-85937-211-2	£14.99	Aug
Worcestershire	1-85937-152-3	£14.99	Aug
Victorian & Edwardian Maritime Album	1-85937-144-2	£17.99	Aug

Available from your local bookshop or from the publisher

FRITH PRODUCTS & SERVICES

Francis Frith would doubtless be pleased to know that the pioneering publishing venture he started in 1860 still continues today. More than a hundred and thirty years later, The Francis Frith Collection continues in the same innovative tradition and is now one of the foremost publishers of vintage photographs in the world. Some of the current activities include:

Interior Decoration

Today Frith's photographs can be seen framed and as giant wall murals in thousands of pubs, restaurants, hotels, banks, retail stores and other public buildings throughout the country. In every case they enhance the unique local atmosphere of the places they depict and provide reminders of gentler days in an increasingly busy and frenetic world.

Product Promotions

Frith products have been used by many major companies to promote the sales of their own products or to reinforce their own history and heritage. Brands include Hovis bread, Courage beers, Scots Porage Oats, Colman's mustard, Cadbury's foods, Mellow Birds coffee, Dunhill pipe tobacco, Guinness, and Bulmer's Cider.

Genealogy and Family History

As the interest in family history and roots grows world-wide, more and more people are turning to Frith's photographs of Great Britain for images of the towns, villages and streets where their ancestors lived; and, of course, photographs of the churches and chapels where their ancestors were christened, married and buried are an essential part of every genealogy tree and family album.
A series of easy-to-use CD Roms is planned for publication, and an increasing number of Frith photographs will be able to be viewed on specialist genealogy sites. A growing range of Frith books will be available on CD.

Frith Products

All Frith photographs are available Framed or just as Mounted Prints, and can be ordered from the address below. From time to time other products - Address Books, Calendars, Table Mats, etc - are available.

The Internet

Already thousands of Frith photographs can be viewed and purchased on the internet. By the end of the year 2000 some 60,000 Frith photographs will be available on the internet. The number of sites is constantly expanding, each focussing on different products and services from the Collection.
Some of the sites are listed below.

www.townpages.co.uk
www.icollector.com
www.barclaysquare.co.uk
www.cornwall-online.co.uk

For more detailed information on Frith companies and products, look at these sites:

www.francisfrith.co.uk
www.frithbook.co.uk
www.francisfrith.com

See the complete list of Frith Books at:

www.frithbook.co.uk

This web site is regularly updated with the latest list of publications from the Frith Book Company Ltd. If you wish to buy books relating to another part of the country that your local bookshop does not stock, you may purchase on-line.

For further information, trade, or author enquiries please contact us at the address below:

The Francis Frith Collection, Frith's Barn, Teffont, Salisbury, Wiltshire, England SP3 5QP.
Tel: +44 (0)1722 716 376 Fax: +44 (0)1722 716 881 Email: uksales@francisfrith.com

To receive your FREE Mounted Print

Mounted Print
Overall size 14 x 11 inches

Cut out this Voucher and return it with your remittance for £1.50 to cover postage and handling.
Choose any photograph included in this book. Your SEPIA print will be A4 in size, and mounted in a cream mount with burgundy rule lines, overall size 14 x 11 inches.

Order additional Mounted Prints at HALF PRICE (only £7.49 each*)
If there are further pictures you would like to order, possibly as gifts for friends and family, acquire them at half price (no additional postage and handling required).

Have your Mounted Prints framed*
For an additional £14.95 per print you can have your chosen Mounted Print framed in an elegant polished wood and gilt moulding, overall size 16 x 13 inches (no additional postage and handling required).

*** IMPORTANT!**
These special prices are only available if ordered using the original voucher on this page (no copies permitted) and at the same time as your free Mounted Print, for delivery to the same address

Frith Collectors' Guild

From time to time we publish a magazine of news and stories about Frith photographs and further special offers of Frith products. If you would like 12 months FREE membership, please return this form.

Send completed forms to:
The Francis Frith Collection, Frith's Barn, Teffont, Salisbury, Wiltshire SP3 5QP

Voucher for FREE and Reduced Price Frith Prints

Picture no.	Page number	Qty	Mounted @ £7.49	Framed + £14.95	Total Cost
		1	**Free of charge***	£	£
			£7.49	£	£
			£7.49	£	£
			£7.49	£	£
			£7.49	£	£
			£7.49	£	£
Please allow 28 days for delivery			* Post & handling		£1.50
Book Title			**Total Order Cost**		**£**

Please do not photocopy this voucher. Only the original is valid, so please cut it out and return it to us.

I enclose a cheque / postal order for £ ....
made payable to 'The Francis Frith Collection'
OR please debit my Mastercard / Visa / Switch / Amex card

Number ....

Expires .... Signature ....

Name Mr/Mrs/Ms ....
Address ....
....
....
....
.... Postcode ....
Daytime Tel No .... Valid to 31/12/01

The Francis Frith Collectors' Guild

Please enrol me as a member for 12 months free of charge.

Name Mr/Mrs/Ms ....
Address ....
....
....
.... Postcode ....